In the Night Sky

Senior Authors

Roger C. Farr

Dorothy S. Strickland

Authors

Richard F. Abrahamson ♦ Alma Flor Ada ♦ Barbara Bowen Coulter

Bernice E. Cullinan ♦ Margaret A. Gallego

W. Dorsey Hammond

Nancy Roser ♦ Junko Yokota ♦ Hallie Kay Yopp

Senior Consultant

Asa G. Hilliard III

Consultants

V. Kanani Choy ♦ Lee Bennett Hopkins ♦ Stephen Krashen ♦ Rosalia Salinas

Harcourt Brace & Company

Orlando Atlanta Austin Boston San Francisco Chicago Dallas New York Toronto London

Theme
IN THE NIGHT SKY

Contents

121 **Theme Opener**

124 **Bookshelf**

Native American Folktale/Social Studies
126 **The Great Ball Game**
retold by Joseph Bruchac
illustrated by Susan L. Roth

Author and Illustrator Features:
Joseph Bruchac and Susan L. Roth

Riddles
142 **Batty Riddles**
by Katy Hall and
Lisa Eisenberg

Nonfiction/Science
146 **Creatures of the Night**
by Judith E. Rinard

Folktale/Science
152 **The Night of the Stars**
by Douglas Gutiérrez
illustrated by María
Fernanda Oliver

Author and Illustrator Features:
Douglas Gutiérrez and
María Fernanda Oliver

Poem
168 **De Koven**
by Gwendolyn Brooks

Art
172 **Art and Literature:**
The Starry Night
by Vincent van Gogh

Nonfiction/Science
174 **Shooting Stars**
by Franklyn M. Branley
illustrated by Holly Keller

Author and Illustrator Features:
Franklyn M. Branley and
Holly Keller

Biography/Science
194 **3–2–1 BLAST-OFF!**

Narrative Nonfiction/Science
200 **Postcards from Pluto**
written and illustrated by
Loreen Leedy

Author Feature: Loreen Leedy

228 **Theme Wrap-Up**

349 **Glossary**

IN THE NIGHT SKY

What do you see when you look at the sky at night? On clear nights, some people look at the moon, stars, and planets. If you go outside, you might also see night animals moving about. The stories you will read will help you learn new things about stars, planets, and animals that are out at night. Then, the next time you look up at the night sky, you may think new thoughts about it.

Theme
IN THE NIGHT SKY

CONTENTS

The Great Ball Game
retold by Joseph Bruchac

Batty Riddles
by Katy Hall and Lisa Eisenberg

Creatures of the Night
by Judith E. Rinard

The Night of the Stars
by Douglas Gutiérrez
translated by Carmen Diana Dearden

De Koven
by Gwendolyn Brooks

Art and Literature:
The Starry Night
by Vincent van Gogh

Shooting Stars
by Franklyn M. Branley

3—2—1 BLAST-OFF!

Postcards from Pluto
written and illustrated by Loreen Leedy

Stellaluna

written and illustrated by
Janell Cannon

Stellaluna, a baby bat, learns
about sharing and caring.

Signatures Library
Award-Winning Author

How Many Stars in the Sky?

by Lenny Hort

One summer night, a boy
and his dad travel to the
country to count the stars.

Signatures Library
Award-Winning Illustrator

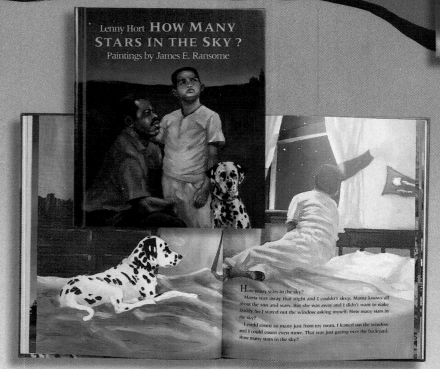

BOOKSHELF

Alistair in Outer Space
by Marilyn Sadler

Space aliens take Alistair on a trip to outer space.

Award-Winning Author

It Came from Outer Space
by Tony Bradman

A class meets a friendly visitor from outer space. There's a surprise ending!

Award-Winning Author

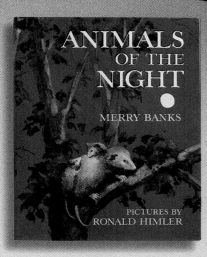

Animals of the Night
by Merry Banks

When everyone is asleep, the night animals are awake—until the sun rises again.

Outstanding Science Trade Book

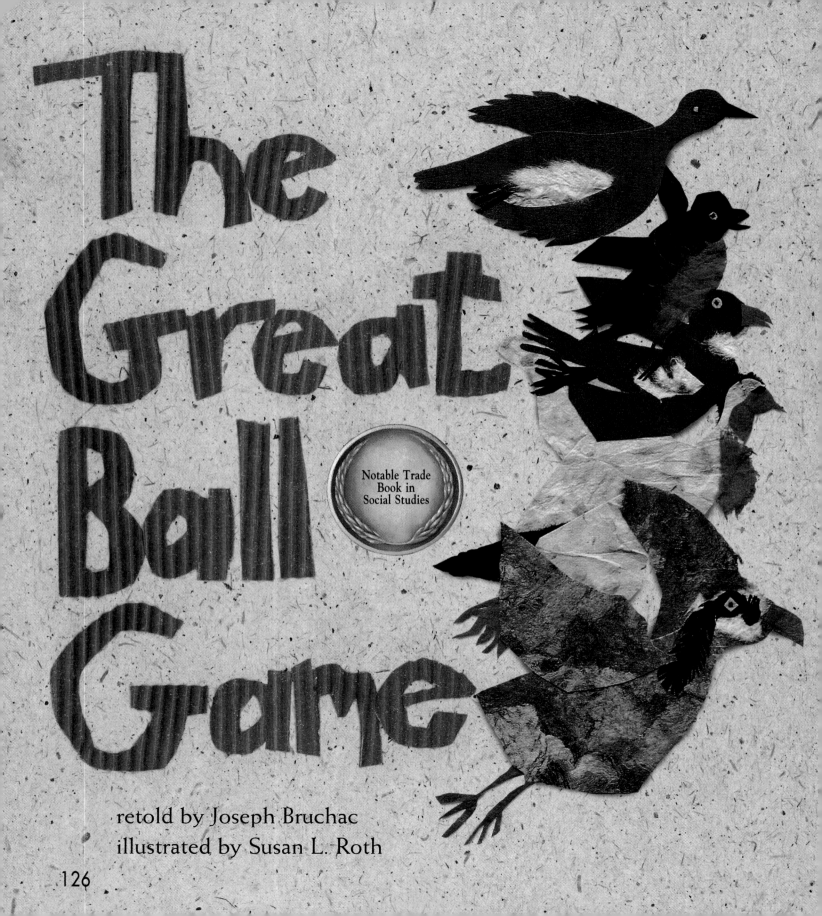

The Great Ball Game

Notable Trade
Book in
Social Studies

retold by Joseph Bruchac
illustrated by Susan L. Roth

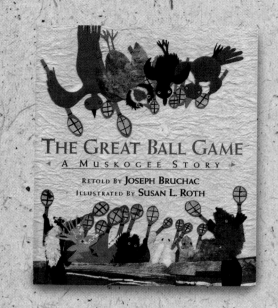

Long ago the Birds and Animals had a great argument. "We who have wings are better than you," said the Birds. "That is not so," the Animals replied. "We who have teeth are better."

The two sides argued back and forth. Their quarrel went on and on, until it seemed they would go to war because of it.

Then Crane, the leader of the Birds, and Bear, the leader of the Animals, had an idea.

"Let us have a ball game," Crane said. "The first side to score a goal will win the argument."

"This idea is good," said Bear. "The side that loses will have to accept the penalty given by the other side."

So they walked and flew to a field, and
there they divided up into two teams.

On one side went all those who had
wings. They were the Birds.

On the other side went those with teeth.
They were the Animals.

But when the teams were formed, one creature was left out: Bat. He had wings *and* teeth! He flew back and forth between the two sides.

First he went to the Animals. "I have
teeth," he said. "I must be on your side."
But Bear shook his head. "It would not
be fair," he said. "You have wings. You must
be a Bird."

131

So Bat flew to the other side. "Take me," he said to the Birds, "for you see I have wings."

But the Birds laughed at him. "You are too little to help us. We don't want you," they jeered.

Then Bat went back to the Animals. "Please let me join your team," he begged them. "The Birds laughed at me and would not accept me."

So Bear took pity on the little bat. "You are not very big," said Bear, "but sometimes even the small ones can help. We will accept you as an Animal, but you must hold back and let the bigger Animals play first."

133

Two poles were set up as the goalposts at each end of the field. Then the game began.

Each team played hard. On the Animals' side Fox and Deer were swift runners, and Bear cleared the way for them as they played. Crane and Hawk, though, were even swifter, and they stole the ball each time before the Animals could reach their goal.

Soon it became clear that the Birds had the advantage. Whenever they got the ball, they would fly up into the air and the Animals could not reach them. The Animals guarded their goal well, but they grew tired as the sun began to set.

Just as the sun sank below the horizon, Crane took the ball and flew toward the poles. Bear tried to stop him, but stumbled in the dim light and fell. It seemed as if the Birds would surely win.

Suddenly a small dark shape flew onto the field and stole the ball from Crane just as he was about to reach the poles. It was Bat. He darted from side to side across the field, for he did not need light to find his way. None of the Birds could catch him or block him.

Holding the ball, Bat flew right between the poles at the other end! The Animals had won!

This is how Bat came to be accepted as an Animal. He was allowed to set the penalty for the Birds.

"You Birds," Bat said, "must leave this land for half of each year."

137

So it is that the Birds fly south each winter. . . .

And every day at dusk Bat still comes flying
to see if the Animals need him to play ball.

139

Joseph Bruchac

Ball games have been played by Native Americans for hundreds of years. Sometimes a ball game was played to settle an argument. The two sides played the ball game instead of going to war.

This story comes from the Muskogee (or Creek) Indians. It is about how the animal people settled an argument with a ball game.

This story was told to Joseph Bruchac by Louis Littlecoon Oliver, a Muskogee Indian in Oklahoma. Bruchac made the game that is played in the story "Stickball," which is like "Lacrosse." Players of this sport have a racket in each hand for scooping up the ball. It is a game that was first played by Native Americans.

Susan L. Roth

Susan Roth used paper from all over the world to make the pictures for this story. The bright red came from an umbrella from Thailand. The dark red came from an envelope from Tibet. Some blue came from Japan and some dark green from Italy.

To make a picture, Susan Roth first lays out all the pieces on a sheet of paper. Then, she moves things around until it's just right. Finally, she glues the pieces down.

Susan Roth makes pictures for stories that come from all over the world. Some are Native American tales. Some are from Africa or India. She likes to make her pictures look like the art that the people in the story would make.

Susan L. Roth

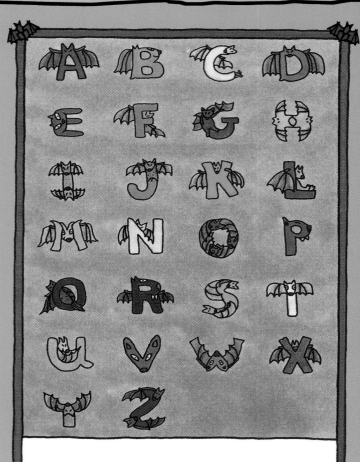

Which bat hangs the highest?

The acro-bat!

Which bat knows its ABCs?

The alpha-bat!

BATTY

written by Katy Hall and Lisa Eisenberg

Why did the baseball player strike out?

He was using the wrong bat!

When do bats squeak?

When they need to be oiled!

RIDDLES
pictures by Nicole Rubel

Tell a Tale with Pictures

Some Native Americans wrote stories using only pictures. Work together to retell "The Great Ball Game" in pictures. Paint your pictures on a big sheet of paper.

You will need:

mural paper, paint, paintbrushes

1. Plan who will paint each part of the story.

2. Paint pictures to tell the story. Use the pictures in "The Great Ball Game" for ideas.

3. Tell the story aloud, using the pictures.

4. Invite another class to hear your tale.

Response

Give Us a Cheer!

A great ball team needs a great cheer!
Work with a group. Choose Birds or
Animals and make up a cheer for your
team. When you are ready, you can
teach your cheer to the others.

What Do You Think?

- Why did it seem like the Birds would win?
  How did Bat help the Animals?
- Would you rather play for the Birds or the
  Animals? Why?

Corner

145

CREATURES
— OF THE —
NIGHT

by Judith E. Rinard

In the evening, as it grows dark, raccoons go down to a river. They are hunting for food in the water.

Raccoons sleep during the day. But at night they wake up and are hungry. A baby raccoon slips, and almost falls. Another raccoon catches a frog and eats it.

There are many animals, like raccoons, that come out when the sun goes down. They are creatures of the night.

Flying Fox

Bats are not birds. They are the only mammals that can fly. This horseshoe bat searches for insects to eat. It catches insects in the air by scooping them up in its wide wings. All day, bats, called flying foxes, hang upside down in a tree. In the evening, they will fly off and look for fruit to eat.

Horseshoe Bat

Long-nosed bats feed on nectar from flowers. One laps up the sweet juice with its long tongue. The other bat pokes its head deep inside a cactus flower. Maybe it is after the very last drop of nectar.

Sanborn's Long-Nosed Bats

149

A flying squirrel leans out of a hole in a tree. It leaves its cozy nest when the sun goes down. Then it leaps from a high branch and spreads the flaps of skin between its front and hind legs. The flaps are like a little parachute. They help the squirrel glide down through the air.

Two squirrels peek out of their home. A third squirrel sits outside and nibbles on a nut.

A mother opossum carries her babies to a tree. The night is almost over. Day is coming, and it is time for the opossum family and other creatures of the night to go to sleep. All night, while you are sleeping, many animals are wide awake.

Isn't the world of the night a busy place?

151

The Night of the Stars

Douglas Gutiérrez
María Fernanda Oliver
Translated by Carmen Diana Dearden

Long, long ago, in a town that was
neither near nor far, there lived a man
who did not like the night.

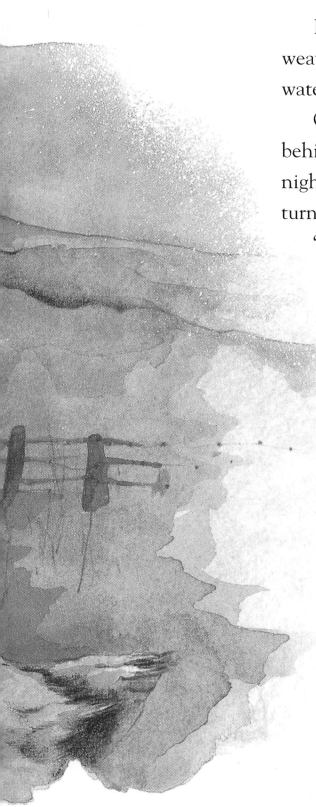

During the day, in the sunlight, he worked weaving baskets, watching over his animals and watering his vegetables.

Often he would sing. But as soon as the sun set behind the mountain, this man who did not like the night would become sad, for his world suddenly turned gray, dark and black.

"Night again! Horrible night!" he would cry out.

He would then pick up his baskets, light his lamp and shut himself up in his house. Sometimes he would look out the window, but there was nothing to see in the dark sky. So he would put out his lamp and go to bed.

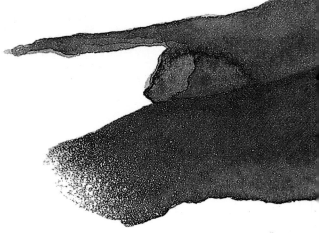

One day, at sunset, the man
went to the mountain. Night was
beginning to cover the blue sky.
The man climbed to the
highest peak and shouted:

"Please, night. Stop!"

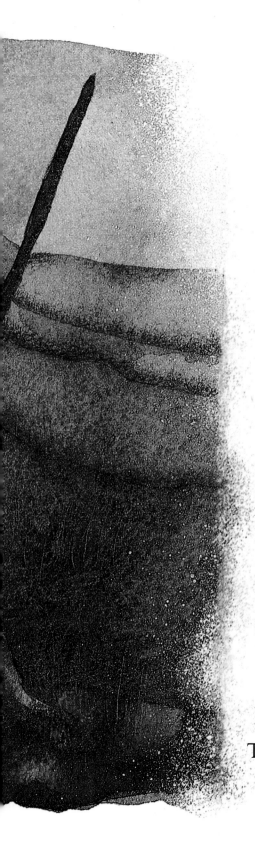

And the night did stop for a moment.

"What is it?" she asked in a soft deep voice.

"Night, I don't like you. When you come,
the light goes away and the colors disappear.
Only the darkness remains."

"You're right," answered the night. "It is so."

"Tell me, where do you take the light?"
asked the man.

"It hides behind me, and I cannot do
anything about it," replied the night.
"I'm very sorry."

The night finished stretching and covered
the world with darkness.

The man came down
from the mountain
and went to bed.

But he could not sleep.
Nor during the next day could he
work. All he could think about
was his conversation with the
night. And in the afternoon,
when the light began to disappear
again, he said to himself:
"I know what to do."

Once more he
went to the mountain.
The night was like an immense
awning, covering all things.
When at last he reached the
highest point on the mountain,
the man stood on his tiptoes,
and with his finger poked a
hole in the black sky.

A pinprick of light flickered
through the hole.
The man who did not
like the night was delighted.
He poked holes all
over the sky.
Here, there, everywhere,
and all over the sky
little points of light appeared.

Amazed now at what
he could do,
the man
made a fist
and punched it
through the darkness.
A large hole
opened up, and a
huge round light,
almost like a grapefruit,
shone through.

All the escaping light cast a brilliant glow
at the base of the mountain and lit up everything below . . .
the fields, the street, the houses.
Everything.

That night, no one in the town slept.

And ever since then, the night is full of lights,
and people everywhere can stay up late . . .
looking at the moon and the stars.

Douglas Gutiérrez

Douglas Gutiérrez lives in Venezuela, South America. He grew up near Caracas, the capital of Venezuela.

Do you like sports? Douglas Gutiérrez does! He was a gym teacher and coach for many years. He coached soccer, gymnastics, softball, and track and field.

The first book Douglas Gutiérrez wrote was about how to be a good sports teacher. *The Night of the Stars* is the first book he wrote for kids.

María Fernanda Oliver

María Fernanda Oliver was born in Venezuela, South America. *The Night of the Stars* is the first story that she has illustrated. The story was first written in Spanish. Now it can be read in English or Spanish.

María Fernanda Oliver painted the pictures with watercolor paints. Her pictures are full of colors and shapes. They are also full of feeling. Did her pictures help you understand how the man felt about the night?

De KOVEN

You are a dancy little thing,
You are a rascal, star!
You seem to be so near to me,
And yet you are so far.

If I could get you in my hands
You'd never get away.
I'd keep you with me always.
You'd shine both night and day.

Gwendolyn Brooks
illustrated by Joanne Scribner

168

169

RESPONSE CORNER

Night and Day

The man in the story did not like the night. Work with a partner to do an experiment about night and day.

1. Get a flashlight and a globe.

2. Put a self-stick note on the globe to show where you live.

3. Find a place that is a little bit dark.

4. One partner shines the flashlight at the globe. The other partner slowly turns the globe.

Then write a note to the man in the story. Draw pictures. Tell what you learned about night and day.

Invent a Night Remover

What might have happened if the man didn't find a way to solve his problem? Work with a partner. Invent a new product to "remove the night." Make a model of it to share with your classmates.

1. Decide what your product will be.

2. Decide how it will work.

3. Make a label that tells the name of your product and how to use it.

You will need:
a clean, empty container
(a box or a plastic bottle)
crayons and markers
scissors
paper and tape

What Do You Think?

• Why did the man poke holes in the sky?

• Did this story change the way you feel about the night? Why or why not?

171

ART & LITERATURE

Pretend that you are walking down a street in the painting. What catches your eye as you look at the sky? How does the painting make you think of starry nights that you have seen?

The Starry Night
by Vincent van Gogh

People all over the world have enjoyed *The Starry Night*. The moon and stars seem to glow. How did Vincent van Gogh make it look as if the stars are moving across the sky?

SHOOTING STARS

Award-Winning
Author

Award-Winning
Illustrator

by Franklyn M. Branley

illustrated by Holly Keller

At night when the sky is clear, look for shooting stars. You can see them as soon as the sky is dark. At first you might not see any. You have to keep looking.

Lie down and gaze at the sky for an hour or so. You're almost sure to see at least one an hour. Maybe you'll see more than one. One time I saw so many, it was hard to count them.

A shooting star is not a star. Long ago people called many things in the night sky some kind of star. When they saw a planet, they called it a wandering star. They called comets long-haired stars. When they saw a streak of light, they thought a star was falling out of the sky. They called it a falling star, or a shooting star. Scientists call them meteors. The word comes from a Greek word meaning "something in the air."

If you could catch a falling star, you would discover that it is a small bit of ash, or solid material like rock or metal. It might be no larger than a grain of sand. It is called a meteoroid. When a meteoroid makes a light streak in the sky, it is called a meteor.

A meteoroid gets very hot. That's because it rubs against the air as it travels toward Earth. It gets hot, just as your hands do when you rub them together.

The meteoroid gets hot enough to produce light. That's the light you see when you see a shooting star.

Many of the meteoroids that fall toward Earth are so small that they don't make a light streak. Or they may fall during the day, when the sky is so bright that we can't see the light streak. Some scientists think that 100 tons of them fall on Earth every day. Most of them fall into the oceans. When you're outside, some of them may fall on you. But you don't feel them, because many are little more than floating specks of dust.

When a meteoroid strikes Earth, the moon, or another planet, it is called a meteorite. Most meteorites are very small. A few are as large as a marble, or even a baseball. Some are very large. One of the largest ever found is in New York City at the American Museum of Natural History. You can see it there. It was found in Greenland, where the Eskimos called it *Ahnighito*—the tent. It is mostly iron, and it weighs more than 34 tons. The Eskimos made iron knives from pieces of this meteorite.

AHNIGHITO

1982

Sometimes meteorites hit houses. In 1982 one that weighed six pounds crashed through the roof of a house in Wethersfield, Connecticut. It was traveling over 1,000 miles an hour. That was fast enough for it to go right through the ceiling and roll under the dining-room table. Eleven years earlier, in 1971, another meteorite went through the roof of a different house in the same town. That one weighed a little less than a pound.

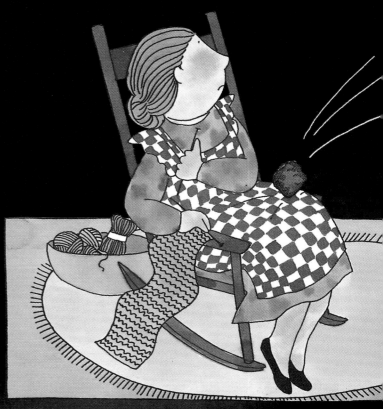

No one was hit by either of those meteorites. But in 1954 Mrs. Hewlett Hodges, who lived in Sylacauga, Alabama, was hit in the thigh by a meteorite that came right through her ceiling. That one weighed about ten pounds. Her thigh was black and blue for quite a while.

1954

Don't worry about being hit by a meteorite. Mrs. Hodges was the first and only person in the United States ever hit by one. In the last 500 years, only a dozen people in the whole world have been hit.

Many meteorites have fallen on buildings. And many have dug deep holes, or craters, in the Earth. This crater is near Winslow, Arizona. It is 4,150 feet wide and 600 feet deep. You can walk around it and climb down to the bottom.

Meteorites have also fallen on the moon. In the picture, you can see that the moon is covered with craters. Many of them were made when large meteorites crashed into the moon long ago.

Mercury and Mars also have lots of craters. Many of them were dug by meteorites.

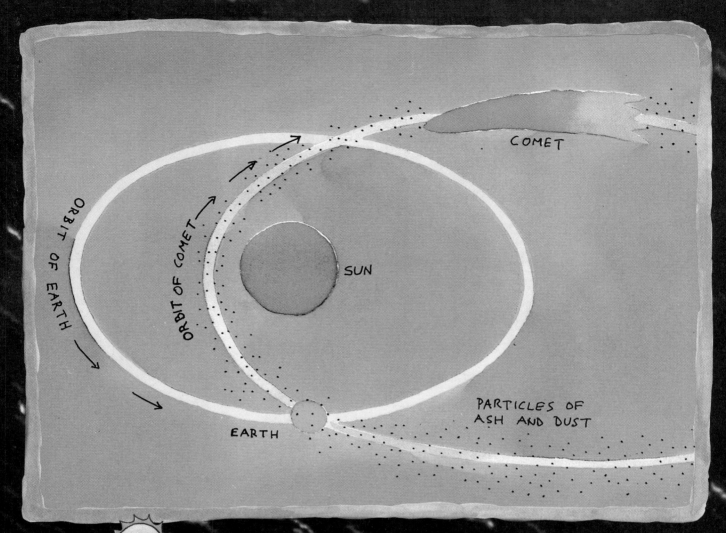

Meteorites are visitors from outer space. Billions of dust particles, stones, and rocks are in orbit around the sun. Some of them have been there since Earth began. Many of the bits of ash and dust were left behind by comets as they traveled through space. When Earth moves through clouds of these particles, they make shooting stars—sometimes so many that they fill the sky.

Keep watching for shooting stars. They seem to be far away, but most of them are less than 60 miles above the Earth. One night you may see one that seems a lot closer. You may be able to trace where it lands. You might even find the meteorite.

That's what happened in Mexico. In 1969 people saw a sky full of shooting stars. Later, almost two tons of meteorites were found by people who saw them land.

1969

Remember, at first when you look into a clear, dark sky you may not see any shooting stars. But keep watching. On a warm night, lie down and gaze at the sky. If you're lucky, you might see three or four every hour.

When you see one, make a wish. Some people say that wishes come true when they are made on a shooting star. Who knows—maybe they are right.

Franklyn M. Branley

When Franklyn Branley was an elementary school teacher, he didn't think there were enough science books for children. He decided to do something about that.

Shooting Stars is just one of over 130 fun science books that he has written. Franklyn Branley knows a lot about shooting stars because he is an astronomer. He has studied stars and planets for years. From his home by the ocean, he has seen many shooting stars.

Holly Keller

As a young person, Holly Keller had two sides—the artist and the serious student. She enjoyed learning about history in college. Later, in an art class, her teacher said that she would be good at drawing pictures for children's books. So that's what she did!

Holly Keller often writes her own stories. This is what happens when she draws pictures for someone else's story. First, someone sends her the words of the story. Then, she gets books so she can learn all about the subject. After that, she draws sketches and sends them to her editor at the book company. She also sends the pictures to an expert who makes sure they are correct. The sketches are sent back and forth until everyone likes them.

Do you know why Holly Keller likes to illustrate science books? She gets to be both an artist and a student, just as she always wanted!

Holly Keller

RESPONSE CORNER

Wish on a Shooting Star

My Pony

Once I wished for a pony.

Then I got a pony. I named him Sneakers.

WRITE A STORY

Write a story about making a wish. Your story can be about you or another character. Tell what happens after the wish is made.

After you write your story, glue it onto star-shaped paper. Add glitter. Make a galaxy of star stories on a classroom wall.

MAKE A BOOK

Make a Question-and-Answer book about meteorites. Each person can write one page.

Write a question about meteorites. Write the answer and draw pictures. Then put everyone's pages together, and think of a good title.

How big are meteorites?

Many meteorites are the size of marbles. → :O: Some meteorites are very big. There is a meteorite in Greenland that weighs more than 34 tons. ↓

What Do You Think?
- What is a shooting star?
- What are three facts about shooting stars that you would tell a friend?

3-2-1 BLAST-OFF!

10-9-8-7-6-5-4-3-2-1-
BLAST-OFF!

There's a burst of bright
light and huge white clouds
as powerful engines lift
the space shuttle toward
the stars.

The astronauts in the space
shuttle are special people.
Meet some of the brave
astronauts who traveled
in space.

Mae Jemison studied hard and became a doctor and a scientist. She also wanted to be an astronaut. When she was a little girl, she always dreamed about going into space. Years later her wish became real. She was chosen from a group of about 2,000 people.

Mae Jemison was the first African American woman to go into space. She blasted off on September 12, 1992, on the space shuttle *Endeavour.*

For fun, Mae Jemison dances and collects African art. Also, she appeared on the television show *Star Trek: The Next Generation.*

Franklin R. Chang-Diaz was born in Costa Rica. Studies about space have always been important to him. As a scientist and an engineer, he is trying to invent ways to help people travel to the planet Mars in the future.

In May 1980 Franklin Chang-Diaz was chosen to become an astronaut. His first launch into space was on January 12, 1986, on the space shuttle *Columbia*.

Robert L. Crippen became a pilot in the United States Navy. Then he became an astronaut. Robert Crippen was in the first space shuttle that lifted off into space in April 1981. He went up into space three more times after that. He was the commander of the flights. Now he is one of the people in charge of the space shuttle program.

197

Leroy Chiao was born in the United States. His parents are from China. He became an engineer because he was interested in science. Later he traveled to China to teach.

Leroy Chiao always wanted to do more. He is helping to build parts for future space telescopes that will help us to see different objects in space.

In July 1991 Leroy Chiao became an astronaut. He blasted off into space on July 8, 1994, on the space shuttle *Columbia*. The shuttle stayed in space for 15 days and traveled around the Earth 236 times!

Sally K. Ride is from California. She was a science teacher. Later she became an astronaut.

Sally Ride was the first American woman in space. She launched into space on the space shuttle *Challenger* in June 1983. Sally Ride went up into space again one year later. This time another woman astronaut went, too. She got the chance to be the first woman to walk in space. And she did!

Charles Bolden, Jr. became a pilot in the United States Marine Corps. Sometimes he flew planes with brand-new engines and parts to make sure the planes were ready to fly. Because of his training as a pilot, Charles Bolden, Jr. became an astronaut in August 1981. His first trip in space on January 12, 1986, was on the space shuttle *Columbia*. He flew in space three more times. His last flight was special because it was the United States' first mission with Russia. Today Charles Bolden, Jr. is a General.

POSTCARDS FROM PLUTO

A TOUR OF THE SOLAR SYSTEM

Award-Winning Author

written and illustrated by
LOREEN LEEDY

comet

Jupiter

Saturn

Uranus

Neptune

Pluto

I see nine planets!

Four of them are much bigger than Earth.

RAY

LIN

THE SOLAR SYSTEM for $1000

TANISHA

SIMON

203

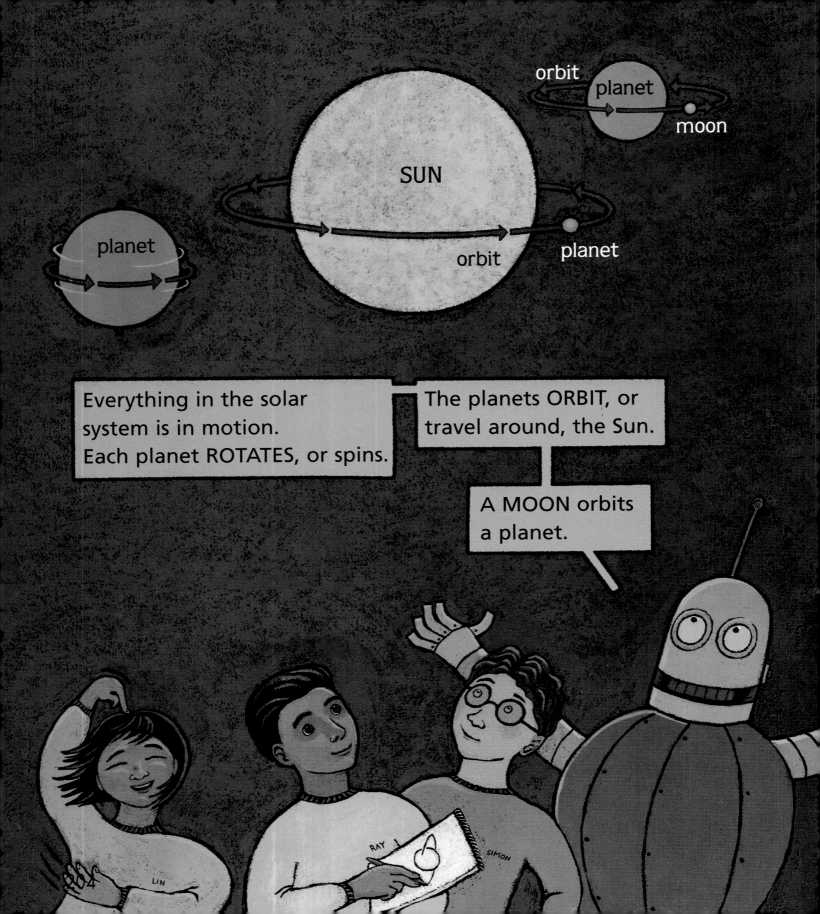

205

First we'll fly by the biggest, hottest, brightest object in the solar system— the Sun.

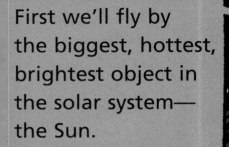

THE SUN

Dear Mom & Dad,
    Did U know that R Sun is really a ☆? It is only a medium-sized ☆, but over 1 million Earths could fit inside. We can't 🐝 2 close because of the intense heat (<u>millions</u> of degrees!)
    Stay cool— Your ☀,
    Ray

Mr. + Mrs. Sol Corona
93 Shady Lane
Sun Valley, Idaho
U.S.A.   83353

P.S. The Sun has darker, cooler blotches called SUNSPOTS.

The bowl-shaped holes on a planet or moon are called CRATERS.

Wow! MERCURY is covered with them.

c

MERCURY

Dear Uncle Freddy,
  GUESS THE PLANET—
  1) It's closest to the Sun.
  2) It has the shortest
     year (88 Earth days.)
  3) It has no water,
     no air, and no moons.
  If you said Mercury,
you're right! Also, it
is burning hot on the
sunny side, and freezing
cold on the dark side.
Good-bye for now!
        Your nephew,
        Eric

Freddy Fickle
100 Quicksilver Dr.
Frozenfire, Alaska
              99552

I'm hot & cold at the same time!

Sunlight

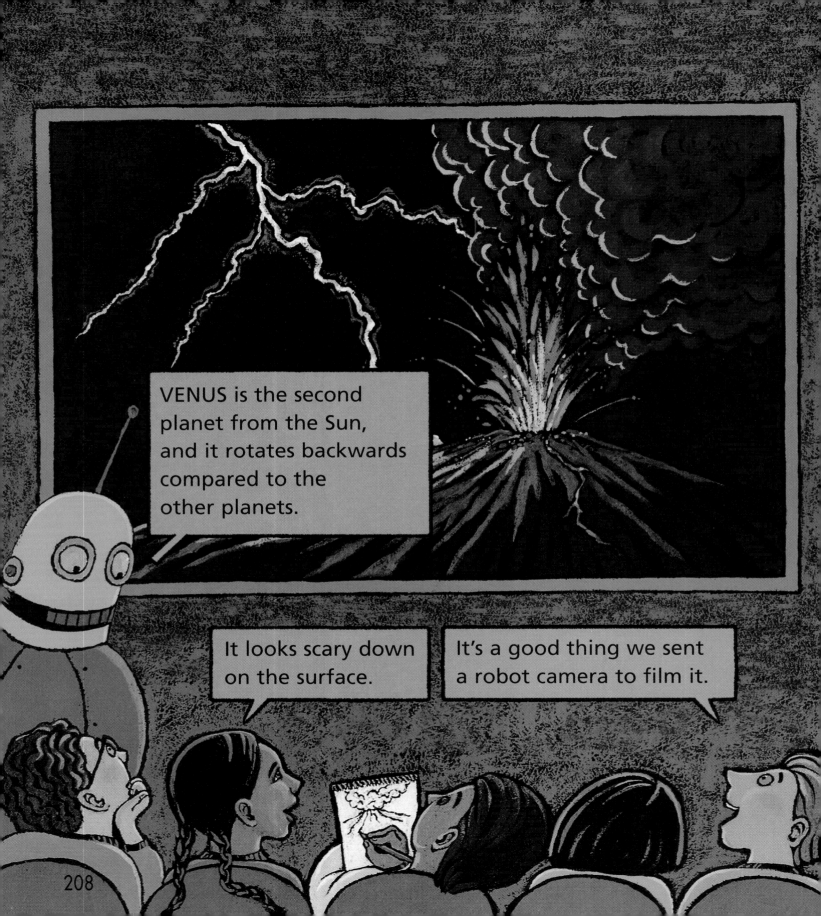

Dear Debbie,
    We saw Venus today, and it's a little smaller than Earth, but much more dangerous. It is covered with thick, poisonous, acid clouds. The air has enough heat and pressure to crack spaceships! Venus has lots of earsplitting thunder, and lightning, too.
    Wish you were here!
        Your friend,
        Simon

Debbie DeMilo
201 Flytrap St.
Cupid City, NY
            12420

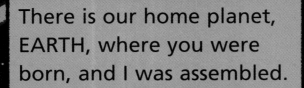

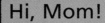

EARTH

MOON

Dear Mom,
    Guess what? We saw the actual footprints of the first astronaut to walk on Earth's moon–Neil Armstrong. We left our footprints, too.   They'll last forever because there's no wind or rain to destroy them. I guess a meteor might crash down on them. That's how the moon's craters were made. I hope a meteor doesn't land on us!
            Love,
                Tanisha
P.S. On Earth I weigh 72 pounds– here I weigh only 12!

Luna Cee
100 Crescent Ave.
Crater Lake, OR
U.S.A. 97604

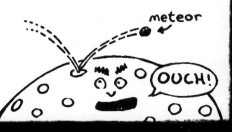

meteor

OUCH!

Earth

MARS

Dear Uncle Martin,
   Here is a poem about Mars—
<u>RED PLANET</u>
Canyons,
Volcanoes,
Clouds of dust,
Boulders,
Craters,
The color of rust.
Scientists think Mars
used to have water in
rivers or oceans. It still
has ice at the poles, but
it's a desert planet now.
   See you!   Love,
          Lin

P.S. Mars has 2
small moons.

Mr. Martin Greenman
#4 Canal Street
Venice, FL
U.S.A.   33595

I am so thirsty!

Look at the thousands of asteroids we're passing. The asteroid belt is between the small, rocky inner planets and the giant outer planets.

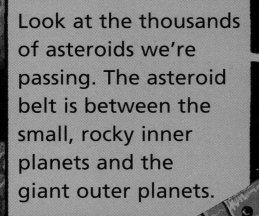

ASTEROID

Dear Mom and Dad,
   Dr. Quasar says that asteroids are big chunks of rock. Most of them stay in the asteroid belt, but one could drift out of orbit and crash into a planet (even Earth!)
                  Love,
                     Simon
P.S. Don't bother wearing helmets—the chance of an asteroid hitting Earth is very small.

Mr. and Mrs. Goldbloom
1000 Collision Road
Bumpers, NJ
U.S.A. 08857

Oh no!

EARTH

JUPITER is made of gases and liquids that swirl around. It has the GREAT RED SPOT which is really a huge storm.

Dear Stella,
  Did U know that Jupiter is the BIGGEST planet? It has colorful stripes, + a very faint ring system made of dust. think the weirdest thing is that has no solid crust of land. Maybe it is sort of like melted !
C U later... Your bro,
    Ray
P.S. has 16 's.

Stella Corona
93 Shady Lane
SunValley, Idaho
U.S.A. 83353

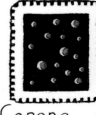

JUPITER

SATURN'S hundreds of rings look solid from a distance, but they are made mostly of many small pieces of ice.

Dear Mom and Dad,
    Here is a poem for you~
SATURN'S RINGS
Snowballs
And icebergs
Drifting in space
Around the planet
The icy chunks race.

    I think Saturn is the prettiest planet. It has more than 20 moons (scientists keep finding new ones!) Love, Lin

Mr. and Mrs. Chang
808 Circle Court
Loopdeloop, CA
U.S.A.   90287

SATURN

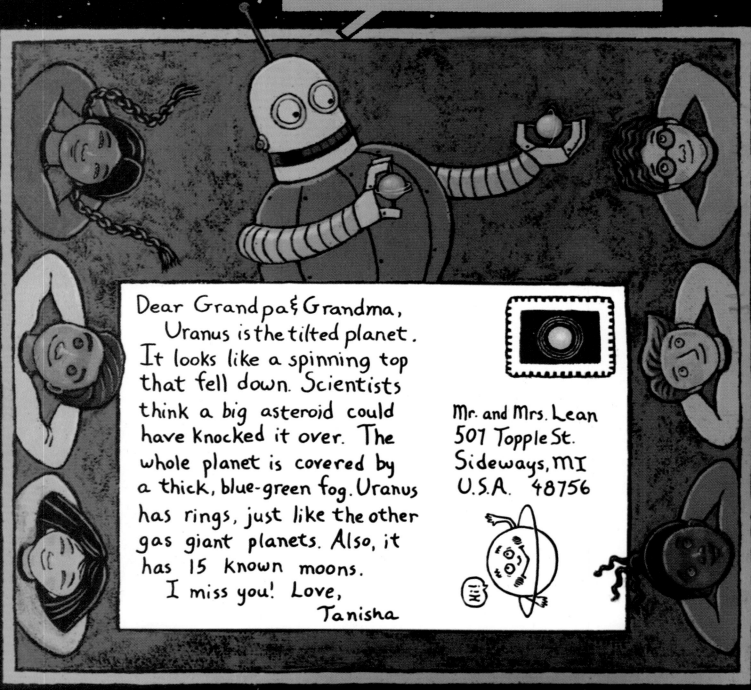

URANUS

Here is PLUTO, the outermost planet.

The Sun looks so tiny from here!

That's why the outer planets are so cold.

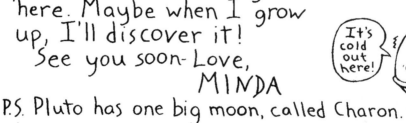

Dear Grandfather,
    Can you believe it—
we are 6 billion kilometers
from home! Pluto is the
very smallest planet, and
the last one in the solar
system (as far as we know.)
Scientists think another
planet could be hiding out
here. Maybe when I grow
up, I'll discover it!
    See you soon—Love,
        MINDA
P.S. Pluto has one big moon, called Charon.

PLANET X?

Joe Thunderhawk
248 Final Trail
Tail End, TX
U.S.A. 77050

It's cold out here!

Charon

PLUTO

It's time to head back to Earth. I hope you all enjoyed your tour of the solar system.

Dear Mom & Dad,
    Here Ⓡ some of the space words 👁 learned:
ASTEROID- space rock
COMET- chunk of frozen gas & dust
CRATER- circular hollow
GALAXY- huge group of stars
MOON- it orbits a planet
ORBIT- to travel around
PLANET- it orbits a star
ROTATE- to spin
STAR- it gives off heat and light
👀 want to visit another galaxy next, okay? ♡ Ray

Mr. + Mrs. Sol Corona
93 Shady Lane
Sun Valley, ID
U.S.A. 83353

POSTCARDS FROM LOREEN LEEDY

Dear Space Traveler,

When I wrote Postcards from Pluto, I read all I could about our solar system. Then I decided which facts were most important. All the information had to fit on postcards like this one.

I drew the pictures for this story, too. When I make a book, I read, write, and draw pictures at about the same time. Sometimes what I write changes what I draw. Sometimes what I draw changes what I write.

I used a robot character to tie together all the facts. My robot has been around for a long time. He came from a book of mine that was never published. He just seemed like the perfect character for this story.

Happy reading!

Loreen Leedy

RESPONSE CORNER

Planets with
Personality
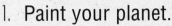

Look at the postcards in the story. The planets are drawn to look like people. Choose one of the planets. Paint it to look like a person. Then have a Parade of Planets.

At the end of the parade, each of you can tell your classmates about your planet.

You will need:

paints and brushes
water pan
markers or crayons
construction paper
scissors
glue or tape

1. Paint your planet.
2. Cut out the planet.
3. Add things to make the planet look like a person.

226

WRITE IN CODE

Write **Like Ray**

Look at the postcards that Ray sent.
He sometimes drew pictures of things instead
of writing words. Think of a short message you want to
send to a friend. First, write the message in words.
Write it again using pictures for some of the
words. Then, give it to your friend to read.

What Do You Think?

- What new things did you learn about the solar system?
- Which planet was the most interesting to you? Why?

THEME
WRAP-UP

You probably know a lot more about planets, stars, and night animals than you did before you read these stories!

- What is the most interesting thing you learned about the night?

- If you could visit a place in our solar system, where would you go? Tell why.

ACTIVITY CORNER

One of the stories you read tells why bats come out when the sun goes down. Another story tells how the moon and stars came to be in the night sky. Think of something you learned about the night. Make up a story that tells why or how this part of the night came to be.

Using the Glossary

▶Get to Know It!

The **Glossary** gives the meaning of a word as it is used in the story. It also has an example sentence to show how to use the word. A **synonym,** or word that has the same meaning, sometimes comes after the example sentence. The words in the **Glossary** are in ABC order, also called **alphabetical order.**

▶How to Use It!

If you want to find *brilliant* in the **Glossary,** you should first find the **B** words. **B** is near the beginning of the alphabet, so the **B** words are near the beginning of the **Glossary.** Then you can use the guide words at the top of the page to help you find the entry word *brilliant.* It is on page 351.

This guide word is the first word on the page.

This guide word is the last word on the page.

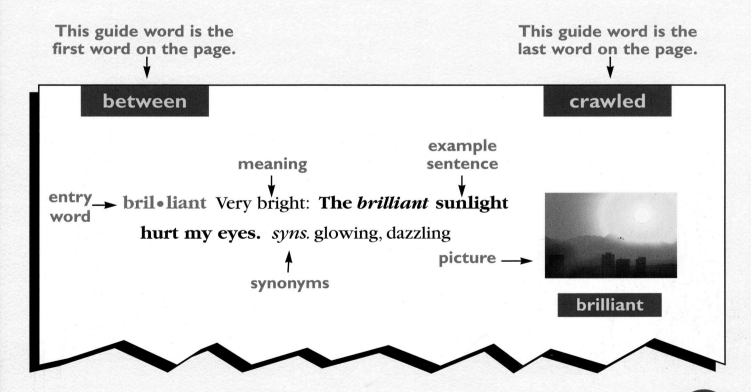

between

crawled

meaning

example sentence

entry word → **bril•liant** Very bright: **The *brilliant* sunlight hurt my eyes.** *syns.* glowing, dazzling

synonyms

picture →

brilliant

A

aboard

a•board Riding on things like ships, planes, and trains: **The people *aboard* the ship waved to the people back on land.**

ac•cept To put up with; to take: **Please *accept* this cake as my way of saying I'm sorry.**

ad•van•tage Something that helps one team do better than the other: **Our basketball players were taller, so we had the *advantage*.**

argue

al•read•y Before a certain time: **We have *already* eaten dinner, so we aren't hungry.**

an•nounced Told others: **She *announced* the winner of the contest.**

ar•gue To give reasons for or against something: **Sometimes my sister and I *argue* about who is right.** *syns.* disagree, fight

ar•gu•ment A fight with words: **Casey had an *argument* with his friend about who was faster.** *syns.* fight, quarrel

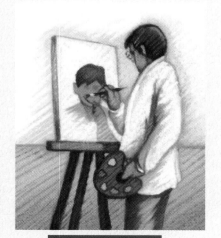

artist

art•ist A person who draws or paints: **The *artist* drew a picture of me.**

B

be•tween In the middle: **I sit *between* Simon and Isabel at school.**

blind•ing Making something hard to see: **The snow was so *blinding* that I couldn't see the house across the street.**

bril•liant Very bright: **The *brilliant* sunlight hurt my eyes.** *syns.* glowing, dazzling

brilliant

brook A very small river: **Mom lets us play in the *brook* because the water is not deep.** *syn.* stream

bus•y Having a lot to do; working: **I was so *busy* doing my homework that I forgot my baseball practice.**

brook

buy To use money to get something: **We *buy* food at the store.**

C

cou•ple Two people together: **The *couple* sat side by side on the bench.** *syn.* pair

cov•er To hide by moving in front of: **Clouds *cover* the sun in a storm.**

couple

crawled Moved slowly: **The cars *crawled* along the crowded city street.**

351

D

dan•ger•ous Not safe: **It can be *dangerous* to cross the street without first looking both ways.**

de•li•cious Tasting or smelling good: **I love the taste of those *delicious* cookies!** *syn.* tasty

de•light•ed Very happy: **I am *delighted* that you can come to my party.** *syn.* pleased

de•stroy To wreck; to ruin: **An earthquake can *destroy* a city.** *syn.* smash

dikes Walls to keep out water: ***Dikes* were built along the river to keep the water from flooding the town.**

dis•ap•pear To go away or become hidden: **We saw the train *disappear* into the tunnel.** *syn.* vanish

dough Flour mixed with water and other things: **Uncle Ralph put the bread *dough* into a pan to bake.**

draw To make a picture: **Will you *draw* a horse for me?**

dough

F

fair Giving everyone the same chance: **The game is *fair* because everyone has a chance to win.**

fam•i•ly A group of people who are related to one another: **My *family* and I eat breakfast together.**

fi•nal•ly At last; at the end: **Ben *finally* finished his story, one week after he started it.**

flood•ed Covered with water: **After it rained, people could not drive on the *flooded* streets.**

G

goes Leaves: **When the sun comes out, the snow *goes* away.**

grown Become larger: **Jake has *grown* two inches since last year.**

guide A person who shows others where to go: **A *guide* showed us the way to the monkey cages.**

H

hor•ri•ble Very bad: **The food tasted *horrible*, so he would not eat it.** *syn.* awful

hours Sixty minutes: **I'm in school for five *hours* each day.**

family

353

instrument

I

in•stru•ment Something you make music on: **Would you like to play an _instrument_ in the band?**

J

jeans Strong cloth pants: **Maggie wore _jeans_ to the school picnic.**

L

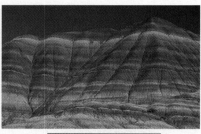

layers

larg•er Bigger: **My dad is _larger_ than I am, so he wears bigger clothes.**

lay•ers Parts that lie one on top of the other: **The baker put icing between the _layers_ of the cake.**

M

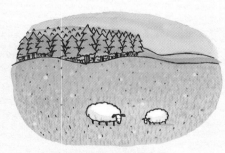

meadow

mead•ow A piece of land where grass grows: **We took the sheep to the _meadow_ to eat the grass.** _syns._ field, pasture

min•ute Sixty seconds; a short amount of time: **I held the frog for a _minute_ and then let it go.**

mouth•ful As much as can fit in a mouth: **Tomiko ate another _mouthful_ of rice.**

354

mu•sic Sounds you play on instruments or sing: **I like the** *music* **the band plays.**

N

new Not old: **Miguel got a** *new* **toy truck for his birthday.**

O

o•ceans Salt water that covers much of the earth: **Ships cross the** *oceans* **to go from one part of the world to another.** *syn.* seas

P

paintings

paint•ings Painted pictures: **Myra used red, yellow, and blue paints to make her** *paintings*.

pit•y A feeling of caring about someone who feels bad: **Peter felt** *pity* **for the boy who hurt his knee.**

plan•et A large, round body that goes around the sun: **The rocket flew around the** *planet* **Mars.**

planet

po•em A group of sentences that often rhyme and that tell about thoughts and feelings: **Keneesha used the words <u>hop</u>, <u>flop</u>, and <u>stop</u> in her** *poem* **about a frog.**

presents

pound•ed Hit very hard: **The man *pounded* the nail into the wood with a hammer.**

pres•ents Things people give to one another: **Kyle got many *presents* on his birthday.** *syn.* gifts

pro•duce To make: **That factory can *produce* many new cars each day.**

Q

quar•rel A fight: **They had a *quarrel* about who would ride the bike first.** *syn.* argument

R

real Not make-believe; not fake: **Rosa read a story about a castle and then visited a *real* one.**

rel•a•tives People in a family: **I like to visit Grandma, Grandpa, and my other *relatives*.**

re•plied Said something to answer a question: **Eddie *replied* "Yes" to the teacher's question.**

S

sea•son A certain time of year: **Summer is our hot *season*.**

se•cure Safe: **During the storm, we felt warm and** *secure* **in our house.**

shoul•der A part of the body, at the top of the arm: **Jan carried the bag over her** *shoulder.*

shove A hard push: **He gave the toy car a** *shove* **to start it rolling.**

show•er A short rain: **There was a light** *shower* **at the park, but I didn't get wet.**

shrieked Yelled in a high voice: **My aunt** *shrieked* **when the mouse ran across the floor.**

sil•ly Foolish; funny: **It would be** *silly* **to keep ice cream in a lunch box.**

slow•ly In a way that is not fast: **Kent was tired, so he walked** *slowly* **down the street.**

so•lar sys•tem The sun, the planets and their moons, and other things that go around the sun: **Jupiter is the largest planet in our** *solar system.*

squawked Made a loud noise like a parrot: **The bird** *squawked* **at us when we got too close.**

stom•achs More than one belly: **Our** *stomachs* **were full from dinner.**

shoulder

shower

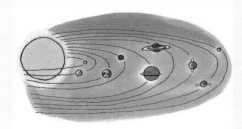
solar system

357

strange Not seen or heard of before: **We ate *strange* food when we went to a country far away.**

stretch•ing Growing: **The fog was *stretching* over the city.** *syn.* spreading

T

tend

talk•ing Speaking: **The boys were *talking* to each other on the phone.**

tend To take care of: **Let's *tend* the garden so that the vegetables will grow.**

thought Believed; felt: **Angie *thought* it was a beautiful day.**

through From beginning to end: **I read *through* the book without stopping.**

thun•der A loud noise made by lightning: **During the storm, we heard loud *thunder*.**

tour A trip to visit a place: **The class saw all kinds of animals on their *tour* of the zoo.**

U

underground

un•der•ground Below the ground: **We walked down steps to get on the *underground* train.**

V

vil•lage A small town: **Marco lives in a *village* near the top of a mountain.**

village

W

weath•er The way things are outside: **Do you like the cool *weather* in November?**

weighs Shows how heavy something is: **That heavy rock *weighs* fifty pounds.**

wom•en Girls who have grown up and now are adults: **Many *women* and men took care of the children.**

women

Acknowledgments

For permission to reprint copyrighted material, grateful acknowledgment is made to the following sources:

Atheneum Books for Young Readers, an imprint of Simon & Schuster: Cover illustration by Ronald Himler from *Animals of the Night* by Merry Banks. Illustration copyright © 1990 by Ronald Himler.

Caroline House, Boyds Mills Press, Inc.: Cover illustration by Maryann Cocca-Leffler from *Wanda's Roses* by Pat Brisson. Illustration copyright © 1994 by Maryann Cocca-Leffler.

Children's Television Workshop, New York: "Family Treasure Chest" from *Kid City Magazine,* May 1994. Copyright 1994 by Children's Television Workshop. "Children of the Land" by Rhetta Aleong, illustration by Manuel King from *Kid City Magazine,* April 1995. Copyright 1995 by Children's Television Workshop.

Dial Books for Young Readers, a division of Penguin Books USA Inc.: Cover illustration by Carol Wright from *It Came from Outer Space* by Tony Bradman. Illustration copyright © 1992 by Carol Wright. *The Great Ball Game,* retold by Joseph Bruchac, illustrated by Susan L. Roth (adapted). Text copyright © 1994 by Joseph Bruchac; illustrations copyright © 1994 by Susan L. Roth. From *Batty Riddles* by Katy Hall and Lisa Eisenberg, illustrated by Nicole Rubel. Text copyright © 1993 by Katy Hall and Lisa Eisenberg; illustrations copyright © 1993 by Nicole Rubel.

Dutton Children's Books, a division of Penguin Books USA Inc.: Cover illustration by the Club de Madres Virgen del Carmen of Lima, Peru from *Tonight Is Carnaval* by Arthur Dorros. Illustration copyright © 1991 by Dutton Children's Books.

Greenwillow Books, a division of William Morrow & Company, Inc.: *Grandfather's Dream* by Holly Keller. Copyright © 1994 by Holly Keller. Cover illustration from *Tomorrow on Rocky Pond* by Lynn Reiser. Copyright © 1993 by Lynn Whisnant Reiser.

Harcourt Brace & Company: Cover illustration from *Stellaluna* by Janell Cannon. Copyright © 1993 by Janell Cannon.

HarperCollins Publishers: *Willie's Not the Hugging Kind* by Joyce Durham Barrett, illustrated by Pat Cummings. Text copyright © 1989 by Joyce Durham Barrett; illustrations copyright © 1989 by Pat Cummings. *Shooting Stars* by Franklyn M. Branley, illustrated by Holly Keller. Text copyright © 1989 by Franklyn M. Branley; illustrations copyright © 1989 by Holly Keller. "De Koven" from *Bronzeville Boys and Girls* by Gwendolyn Brooks. Text copyright © 1956 by Gwendolyn Brooks Blakely.

Holiday House, Inc.: *Postcards from Pluto: A Tour of the Solar System* by Loreen Leedy. Copyright © 1993 by Loreen Leedy. Cover illustration from *Who's Who in My Family?* by Loreen Leedy. Copyright © 1995 by Loreen Leedy.

Henry Holt and Company, Inc.: Cover illustration from *At the Beach* by Huy Voun Lee. Copyright © 1994 by Huy Voun Lee. *The Sun, the Wind and the Rain* by Lisa Westberg Peters, illustrated by Ted Rand. Text copyright © 1988 by Lisa Westberg Peters; illustrations copyright © 1988 by Ted Rand. Cover illustration by Margaret Hewitt from *Pearl Paints* by Abigail Thomas. Illustration copyright © 1994 by Margaret Hewitt.

Just Us Books Inc.: *Annie's Gifts* by Angela Shelf Medearis, illustrated by Anna Rich. Text copyright 1994 by Angela Shelf Medearis; illustrations copyright 1994 by Anna Rich.

Kane/Miller Book Publishers: *The Night of the Stars* by Douglas Gutiérrez, translated by Carmen Diana Dearden, illustrated by María Fernanda Oliver. Originally published in Venezuela in Spanish under the title *La Noche de Las Estrellas* by Ediciones Ekaré-Banco del Libro, 1987. Published in the United States by Kane/Miller Book Publishers, 1988.

Little, Brown and Company: "This Is My Rock" from *One at a Time* by David McCord. Text copyright 1929 by David McCord. Originally published in *The Saturday Review.*

National Geographic Society: From *Creatures of the Night* by Judith E. Rinard. Text copyright © 1977 by National Geographic Society.

Orchard Books, New York: *Shoes from Grandpa* by Mem Fox, illustrated by Patricia Mullins. Text copyright © 1989 by Mem Fox; illustrations copyright © 1989 by Patricia Mullins.

G. P. Putnam's Sons: Too Many Tamales by Gary Soto, illustrated by Ed Martinez. Text copyright © 1993 by Gary Soto; illustrations copyright © 1993 by Ed Martinez.

Scholastic Inc.: Cover illustration by J. Brian Pinkney from *Happy Birthday, Martin Luther King* by Jean Marzollo. Illustration copyright © 1993 by J. Brian Pinkney.

Simon & Schuster Books for Young Readers, a division of Simon & Schuster: The Little Painter of Sabana Grande by Patricia Maloney Markun, illustrated by Robert Casilla. Text copyright © 1993 by Patricia Maloney Markun; illustrations copyright © 1993 by Robert Casilla. Cover illustration by Cecily Lang from *A Birthday Basket for Tía* by Pat Mora. Illustration copyright © 1992 by Cecily Lang. *The Relatives Came* by Cynthia Rylant, illustrated by Stephen Gammell. Text copyright © 1985 by Cynthia Rylant; illustrations copyright ©1985 by Stephen Gammell. Cover illustration from *JoJo's Flying Side Kick* by Brian Pinkney. Copyright © 1995 by Brian Pinkney. Cover illustration by Roger Bollen from *Alistair in Outer Space* by Marilyn Sadler. Illustration copyright © 1984 by Roger Bollen.

Smithsonian Institution Press, Washington DC: Untitled poem (Retitled: "Rainbow Days") by Nootka, translated by Frances Densmore, from Bureau of American Ethnology, Bulletin #124.

Tambourine Books, a division of William Morrow & Company, Inc.: Cover illustration by James E. Ransome from *How Many Stars in the Sky?* by Lenny Hort. Illustration copyright © 1991 by James E. Ransome.

Ticknor & Fields Books for Young Readers, a Houghton Mifflin Company imprint: Cover illustration from *Ruth Law Thrills a Nation* by Don Brown. Copyright © 1993 by Don Brown.

Wordsong, Boyds Mills Press, Inc.: "Families, Families" by Dorothy Strickland and Michael Strickland from *Families,* selected by Dorothy S. Strickland and Michael R. Strickland. Text copyright © 1994 by Dorothy S. Strickland and Michael R. Strickland.

Photo Credits

Key: (t) top, (b) bottom, (c) center, (l) left, (r) right.

Hans & Judy Beste/ Animals Animals, 148(tl); Dennis Brack/Black Star/Harcourt Brace & Company, 141; Courtesy of Franklyn M. Branley, 190; Courtesy of Robert Casilla, 257(t); Steven Dalton/Animals Animals, 148(r)-149(l); Jack Dermid, 150(bl&r), 150(l); Courtesy of Ediciones Ekaré, 167(t), 167(b); Michael Greenlar/Black Star/Harcourt Brace & Company, 140; Harvard College Observatory/ Science Photo Library/ Phot Res. Inc., 178-179; Philip Hayson/ Photo Researchers, Inc., 182-183; Dale Higgins/Harcourt Brace & Company, 91(l); Joe Johnson III, 116; Ken Karp, 170-171, 314, 317; Russ Kinne, 146(r),147(l); Russ Kinne/ Comstock, 150(b); Ron Kunzman/Harcourt Brace & Company, 225; Wayne Lankinen/ Bruce Coleman, Inc., 150(tc); Tom McHugh/ Field Museum Chicago/ Photo Res., 185; NASA, 194-196, 198; Alan G. Nelson/ Animals Animals, 146(l); Pekka Parviainen/ Science Photo Library/ Photo Res. Inc., 174-175, 192-193; Carl Purcell/ Photo Res., Inc., 180-181; Rev. Ronald Royer/ Science Photo Library/ Photo Researchers, Inc., 186-187; Jerry Schad/Photo Researchers, Inc., 188-189; Flip Schulke/ Black Star, 288-289; Joe Sohm/ Photo Res., Inc., 184-185; Mark Souffer/Animals Animals, 151(tc); Tom Sobolik/Black Star/Harcourt Brace & Company, 91(r), 117, 191, 257(b), 345; Tony Star/ World Perspectives, 197; Superstock, 199; John Troha/Black Star/Harcourt Brace & Company, 256; Merlin D. Tuttle/ Photo Res. Inc., 149(br); Steve Woit, 312; Jacqui Wong 318-323; Photos from Cynthia Rylant's autobiography "Best Wishes" copyright © 1992 published by Richard C. Owens Publishers, Inc.; Edward Potthast *A Holiday* (1915), reprinted with permission from *Children's Book Press,* San Francisco, California, 68-69; Vincent van Gogh *The Starry Night* (1889), The Museum of Modern Art, New York, 172-173; Marc Chagall *The Green Violinist (Violoniste)*(1923-24), The Solomon R. Guggenheim Museum, New York, Photograph by David Heald © The Solomon R. Guggenheim Foundation, New York (FN 37.446), 286-287

Illustration Credits

Steve Johnson and Lou Fancher, Cover Art; Gyron Gin, 6-7, 13-17, 68-69, 120; Nathan Jarvis, 8-9, 121-125, 172-173, 228; Mercedes McDonald, 10-11, 229-233, 286-287, 348; Robert Casilla, 234-257; David Coulson, 194(t); Pat Cummings, 100-117; Stephen Gammell, 46-61; Iskra Johnson 174(t); Brenda Joysmith, 62-63; Kid City CTW, 68-69; Holly Keller, 174-191, 324-345; Loreen Leedy, 200-225; Ed Martínez, 70-91; Patricia Mullins, 18-43; María Fernanda Oliver, 152-167; Ted Rand, 290-313; Anna Rich, 262-283; Susan L. Roth, 126-141; Nicole Rubel, 142-143; Joanne Scribner, 168-169; Terry Widener, 258-259; Robert Casilla, 260-261; Pat Cummings 119(br); Susan Detrich, 64-65; Obadinah Heavner, 92-93; Jane Dill, 192-193; Ted Rand 316(t), 317(t&r); Loreen Leedy 226-227; Bonnie Matthews, 118-119; Rita Pocock Laskaro, 144-145; Lisa Pomerantz, 44-45; Anna Rich, 284-285; Scott Scheidly, 170-171, 284-285.